Conner Maikai-St. Louis

SIMPLY RIGHT THERE

Do see it; it is right before your eyes.
Really look and capture the whole view.
Right in front of your face,
simply simple to understand
though the ideology of illusion
makes it all seem complicated and chaotic
giving reason to being in the right place
at the right time
in the right manner.

Darts thrown at everyone
add a bit of complicity
to the ambiguous patterns
and unstable reactions,
and the pain ,
agony , and
humiliation received in a normal lifetime.

Be grateful for overcoming harm,
and say, "Thank you!" for simply
being alive and
for the great privilege
of just breathing in
possibilities that could happen.

2

Take the next step forward,
and the next ,
and the next possible step right now,
that will bring you closer
to being the person you really are.

Robert Uhene Maikai, Editor

Teuta S. Rizaj, professor emeritus, is an award-winning poet, novelist, memoirist, essayist, translator, literary scholar, and a short story writer. Rizaj's poems have also appeared in Savant Poetry Anthology, Shpresa Magazine and elsewhere. Her published works include ON THE WAVES OF LIFE: A Collection of Stories Narrated by Skender E. Rizaj (KDP 2020); THE GIFT TO LOVE: A Memoir of the Life and Legacy of Nazmije Luta Rizaj (KDP 2019); WHO STOLE THE RAINBOW COLORS (Createspace 2017); ALI PASHE TEPELENA NE ROMANET ANGLEZE: Studim Letraro-Shkencor (Ali Pasha of Tepelena in English Novels: A Literary-Scientific Study) (Createspace 2016); THE SLICED LAND AND OTHER STORIES (Createspace 2015); THE RHAPSODY OF THE ANT WOMAN Poem with Complementary Drawings (Createspace 2014).

ODE ON THE PRINCESS KA'IULANI AINAHAU GARDEN

In the heart of a small fenced garden,
squeezed between high-rises by the murky Ala Wai,
the monument of dear Princess there stands;
Alas, not for long! Ask, but why?

Whispers of a memorial service,
by the new sepultures that therein throng,
swim like waves through the quivering leaves,
to catch her peacocks' dying song.

No memorial of any kind will remain,
to tell the place of her Garden she loved.
No remains of a rainbow rising exuberant,
from the sacred depths of the bones rattled.

Uncle, Aunt, Godmother...say not of her,
she didn't let them know of the beholding far:
The ali'i lands are spacious, but greed's so rapacious;
any edifice on her Ainahau Garden shall be black as char.

O the faithfulness of Hawaiian soul, do but vow—
to the royal sacred one: To be the true Preserver,
till all good sense, which most had hidden,
sees this Desecration proceeds no further.

TEARS FOR TREES

Sharp, menacing saw sweeps through the trees;

the torn branches veer downward, and leaves
flounder away in whips of ocean air,
leaving the shore utterly bare.

Money man, he watches with veiled eyes—
the leveled shore lying in front of his new house.
He picks the ways, he cuts the pattern
of our future apocalyptic days.

Tearful, enraged, his neighbors complain:
Cutting down trees from north to south,
east to west, that's what these ungodly money
men famously do the best.

The ocean warns will devour the treeless shore;
and the money man's rooms will turn into swimming
pools, and the couches of gold, whereon he reclines,
perhaps into lifeboats, as he drowns!

WHILE WAITING FOR THE BUS

I met a man the other day, while waiting for
the Bus 23. He came out of the Store ABC,
and on his way to the Hilton Hotel,
he couldn't but stop to greet me.

His job, he said, was to fly those United silver birds,
through white clouds and across blue skies;
over the mountains, seas, and oceans, connecting
lands, national and foreign, from sunset to sunrise.

The blue of his eyes had been borrowed from the skies.
The white of his face, from the clouds and snowy
mountain peaks. The sweetness of his diction, from
all the friendly lands, whose skies he had streaked.

But the honesty of his smile came from his ancient
fatherland lying between two rivers: so cultured,
so advanced, so civilized that the rest of the dark
world had to steal most of its light.

Before my bus arrived, I had time enough to apologize:
for all the civilized ravages to his fatherland we did,
and the darkness we brought to it. As I boarded the bus,
he smiled his honest smile, and blew me a kiss.

GRIEF IS A GHASTLY MESS

Is your heart thoroughly broken, motherless soul?
Or is that just sorrow washing your eyes—
with its morning dew?

Pua La'a Kea -- Sacred Light of Flower

On your desk, Ay, the guide-map of bereavers does lie;
still you're drifting like flotsam on an endless sea—
with no sight of land on the other side of the horizon.

Still lost in those monotonous caverns,
echoing all your thoughts melded together like water—
with no form, no bend, no beginning, no end.

Still bushwhacking your way through tangled foliage of pain,
wondering if the sea or the rain could erode that flinty pain,
yearning, sadness, emptiness—grief is a ghastly mess.

A pin drop away from life lies death.
Four elements combined to yield to the fifth:
So formidable, invincible—wish we could do away with.

From dust, memories rise to twist my throat into a corkscrew:
When the shades of wintery evening began to close in upon
her, and in one swoop, all her roses were torn up by the root.

How can I forget her face illuminating as it was;
the rhythms of her saintly voice ringing in my ears;
her heart that loved with no pause, no reason, no cause!

Wish I could go back to yesterday, when she was still alive;
back to yesterday, when I could still hold her earthside;

when she was my anchor, my pillar, my life's lullaby.

Oh, this soul of mine, so happy once from sole to crown;
now trampled underfoot of grief like a lifeless seed.
Where can such a soul find solace, some peace?—

In the dreams that rise to caress the sky and kiss her lips?
By a bitter stagnant pond, or a sweet rolling river?
Amidst the jungle's cacophony, or serene green valley?

Wooded dells of silver lime, burned by fire and by frost,
or in those skillful hands of shaman Time?—
For no spoke on the Wheel of life and death is ever lost.

MESSENGER 2020

for Sufi Master Fariha, my endless source of inspiration

I've come as a fresh and fruity messenger—
just ripe for the 2020 seasons, and beyond,
in hues of red, gray-cream, and tangerine.

When the one who sings the song spoils the song;
is it not they can spoil you too? When the things you love
are taken; is it not they were never yours at all?
When the fragrance of "the wise man" departs you;

is it not all crisis points of history begin with human frailty?

Much is ruined in pursuit of power and wealth;
now under their broken spell,—
you stand exposed as very far from strong.
A deep disquiet I sense in each and every soul,
and if I offer you solace, I feel bound to do so.

Your life is defined not by what you let go,
but what you let in: Humanship and kind deeds,
common decency and sensitivity.

What marks the start of any new reality?—
It's where you relearn to look inside into the cabinet
of your soul and mind, and set aside of ego batter.
It's where you relearn to preserve the beauty and force
of truth, and diffuse its essence as an attar.

It's where you let the four chambers reconceive
the exquisite ways to care and to give. It's where you
become more conscious about environment, health,
and hygiene. It's where you make your mistakes,
make amends, and forgive.

It's hard to put down a chilling thought:
"Maybe this pandemic is never going to end."

Fear, which now pervades the hearts,
like a soft and pliable nitrile glove, takes the shape
and size of the hand that's put into it.

The asset is knowing that the present will eventually pass,
and what do you leave behind you when the future calls,
and that the way you embrace it has the power to change:
Everything.

The life that matters is never the life itself,
but rather what you make of it:
What you allow to thrive, or to rot and die.

In walking with Me, you shall be like a tree, planted
by the rivers of mercy; that bears fruit in the right
season, so you're blessed with a new bountiful life.

Nothing is ever beyond repair—
you break, you fall, and you start again.
Shattered hearts can be mended,
businesses can be resurrected, jobs restored.
Trust shoots can burgeon amid the broken stone.

Yes, you may say I'm a phantom, invisible, spooky;
doubting my purpose while hoping for the sun's rays to
burnish the stay-at-home walls, and mellow the sorrows;

In the cracks between the contagious corpses,
seeds to burst into flower. And among the PPE rubble,
primrose and speedwell to bloom, as they did in
the wake of the Black Death and the Spanish Flu.—
Lo! every human plague is different until it's the same.

Abhor me not: I've come as an invaluable aid
to your spiritual labor.—To guide you through
dark passage that gives great illumination.
You named me COVID-19, a vicious coronavirus;
I'm in fact a Messenger, your benevolent helper.

And so, you see, the humanity's next chapter starts
not with me, but with you. I shall say no more,
for that's all I can tell you; that's all you need to know.

Robert Uhene Maikai, Editor

14

Yuan Hongri is a renowned Chinese mystic, poet, and philosopher. His work has been published in the USA, UK, India, New Zealand, Canada, and Nigeria; his poems have appeared in ALOHA LA'A KEA (2020 Savant Poetry Anthology) as well as Poet's Espresso Review, Orbis, Tipton Poetry Journal, Harbinger Asylum, The Stray Branch, Acumen, Pinyon Review, Taj Mahal Review, Madswirl, Shot Glass Journal, Amethyst Review, The Poetry Village, and other e-zines, anthologies, and journals. His best known works are "Platinum City" and "Golden Giant." His works explore themes of prehistoric and future civilization.

English Translations by Manu Mangattu, Assistant Professor, Department of English, St George College Aruvithura, India (The Song of the Universe, Day and Night in Kingdom of Heaven, Distant Heaven, The Prehistoric Golden State and Words Such as God) and Yuanbing Zhang (Gold Heaven).

THE SONG OF THE UNIVERSE—THY SONG

Sweet soul,

let thy breath be sweet

Let thine eyes shine as the stars

Reflect about what thou shalt see!

Thou shalt forget the words

The song of the universe is thy song

The peace of the universe is thy peace

If thou shall speak

it is almost like God

Let there be light! And there was light.

DAY AND NIGHT IN KINGDOM OF HEAVEN

Last night, gazing at the stars

I saw those countless gems smiling

numberless from my past life

limitless in the silver kingdom

Sprung from the light of thought

forging ahead to superluminal chi

Five hundred years later, or, may I say

After a thousand five hundred years of the world

I saw a giant of a spacecraft

The eyes of those men and women

were tranquil, serene as a diamond

Then I knew, once and forever: on the new planet,

in the Kingdom of Heaven, there is neither day nor night.

DISTANT HEAVEN

Often I have a foretaste of the future city of the giant
The young giants in and out of the great mansion in platinum
and I'm one of them
In the body the sacred flame burns
on the head flickers the signs of zodiac
and the Diamond eyes glimpse the distant kingdom of heaven!

THE PREHISTORIC GOLDEN STATE

Wish my smile were a golden armour.
May the Sun's golden mirror guard your chest.
In the music of hundreds of millions of stars
Let your dreams sweeten like the wine of dawn.

The gods in heaven, the guardian of your soul
Out of the book of the giant bestow upon you a day
When Mountains bow to greet you, and,
A golden country, in ancient epoch, the ocean confers.

WORDS SUCH AS GOD

Winter comes and winter goes
Until boots back the golden spring.
My soul has boarded the dragon car of Gods
And has just called on the kingdom of 72 planets.

Words such as God, where everyone is king
When their sun blossoms to you, forever
You will forget the world and forget the years.

GOLD HEAVEN

(translated by Yuanbing Zhang)
I.
The golden sidestep of the days,ah!
arranged golden ladders years.
A mirror
let me saw
countless smiles of time.
The long corridors of gold
leading to countless crystal space-times.
On golden gates
carved with the rounds of
golden sun.
I walked into the rounds of
the mirror of the sun

and saw the palaces of gold.
The big birds of gold feathers,ah!
singing the prehistoric stories to me.
I'm the giant in the sun,ah !

I am the golden sun.
Countless centuries ago
I flew in the crystal universe.
To date the magnificent gold palaces
still waiting for me in the sun
To date the golden sun
Singing in the universe.

I am the king of the sun,ah!
The dragon and phoenix are my mounts.
The wheel of the golden sun
It's all my hometown.

The countless golden suns
Laughing at me in the universe.
The huge dragons and phoenixes
Flying in the crystal space.

The golden rivers,ah!
Flying down from the sky
and turned into

the new golden seas of time.

I saw the huge castles,ah!
Standing above the ocean.
In the sky with red clouds wafting
sparkled the colourful lights.

The cities of crystal,ah!
like the lofty mountains in the sky.
The aerial gardens,ah!
like the colorful clouds floating in the sky.

I was riding on a golden dragon,ah!
flew to the golden space,
turned into the golden lights,ah!
and flew into the wheels of the sun.

The golden flames of the sun
like a huge and beautiful wreath.
The sacred temples
Smilling and opening to me.

I saw the giants,ah!
Lived happily in the sun.
Their sweet smiles,ah!
like a beautiful garden.

Their great art,ah!
sparkled the divine joy.
The magnificent palaces of gold,ah!
Were exactly their masterpiece.

The flowers of the jewels and gold,ah!
Were in full bloom in the gardens of the sun.
The pavilions and towers of crystal,ah!
Sparkled the strange light.

The lines of words of jewels
enchased in the walls of gold.
The huge statues
smilling to you gladly.

The massive painting that engraved by gold
hung in the center of the main hall.
Inlaided with gems
like the cities of gold.

The huge dragon and phoenix
singing joyfully in the sky,
like the pieces of mysterious movement
made me to forget the time suddenly.

Every giant sun
was the kingdoms of gold.
The countless holy giants
lived their miraculous lives.

They had neither night
nor years of the world.
Ten million years of mankind
seemed to be their one day.

They had no worry
sparklling the light all over their bodies,
like the rounds of sun
smiled gladly all the time.

Their divine wisdom
could change the universe,
Let every star in the sky
to turn into the beautiful home.

Countless hundreds of millions of years ago
they created humans.
Even the little earth
was also their works.

With their own spirits

they created the universes.
The countless shining stars
like their words.

In that distant space
they were engaged in creation.
The whole change of minkind
has already existed in their eyes.

They were the ancestors of mankind
And were filled with affections to mankind,
and all the wisdom of mankind
had come from their transmission.

Many centuries ago
they have come to the world,
created the sacred civilizations
and the cities of gold.

Their offspring from generation to generation
lived and reproduced on the earth,
experienced numerous changes
To have human today.

Those ancient civilizations
are still shining in space.

All the past time
are all in another space.

The prehistoric civilization of mankind
will come fortunately again to the world,
As if the underground seeds
sprout and bloom on the ground.

The countless great arts
will be brilliant youth!
That miraculous science and civilizations
will illuminate the new history.

The old earth,ah!
And will be young again.
The flames of his heart,ah!
Will make himself transparent.

The countless sleeping time,ah!
Will wake up from the stone.
The bright and holy lights
will turn into the springs.

Those holy giants,ah!
Will go out of the sun,
with the wisdom of those lights

Illuminating the time-space of mankind.

The golden halls will appear
in the transparent oceans,
like the giant ships
towards the coast of mankind.

In the silent mountains
will ring out the joyful songs,
the fragrant rivers
will flow into the paradises of mankind.

I opened the doors,ah!
And saw the space-times,
the great civilizations,ah!
laughing before my eyes.

The countless eras of light
are coming up to us.
The cities of crystal
blooming in the new time-spaces.

The great flowers of civilization
blossoming in the seas of time-space.
The rounds of the golden sun
are also laughing and singing in space.

The countless cities of gold
blinking towards me in the sun,
spilt the gay singings
like the colorful flowers.

I saw that heaven and earth
filled with laughters everywhere,
that giant planets
also turned into human homes.

II.
I opened one door after another
And flew into a sun after another.
The sacred golden civilization,ah!
like an endless long corridor of time.

Those giants of the sun,ah!
working on the sacred creation.
Let the gold of time
To turn into the countless paradises

Their holy spirits,ah!
Illuminated the space-times,
and created the magic sciences
and that holy arts.

I heard the rounds of the sun,ah!
Singing to me in space,
as if there were countless suns
sending out the golden lights.

I entered the universes
and opened the time-spaces
Every crystal space,ah!
There were also the rounds of the sun.

The stars of time,ah!
Shining in the space of crystal
turned into the bright lights
and agglomerated into the sea of the universe.

All the wisdom of the world
came from the deep space.
The seas of time,ah!
were pregnant with the countless suns.

All the future of mankind
were enshrined in the sun.
The future pictures of the mankind
Will shine the joyful lights.

Every wanderer of the world
are all the descendants of the sun,
The countless centuries ago,ah!
were all the golden giants.

Opening the picture books of the time,ah!
The mankind had been incomparable tall.
The Himalayas,ah!
Was just a little giant.

Before the birth of the earth
mankind have already existed.
The countless stars of the universe
had all been the human homes.

The changes of mankind,ah!
Created the different civilizations.
The another great space,ah!
determined the course of the world.

The future of mankind has been arranged
in the golden palace of the sun,
as if the huge pictures
were enshrined in the rolls of golden book.

The golden books of the sun

shone the words of gold,
the lines of mysterious words,   ah !

Gestated the future civilization.

All kinds of issues of human creation,   ah !

Came from the revelation of the sun
Only the holy spirit
could understand the words of the sun.

The giants of the sun,ah!
Were the master of the sun.
The rounds of the great suns
were the lights of their hearts.

They were the ancestors of mankind,ah!
They were the earliest human.
In the sun,ah!
Watching their descendants.

I heard their singings
calling me days and nights.
That sweet and moving singing,ah!
were the cups of beautiful wine.

I saw the lines of words,ah!

Shining in the palace of the sun
Their divine wisdom
gave me the limitless comforts.

In the layers of the heavens
they were concomitant with me.
Watching me on the earth
To create the new poems.

Their holy lights
shining in my eyes
Turned into the lines of words
and wrote the new poems.

Their divine wisdom
perpetuated in these poems.
The bright future of mankind
turned into the pictures

I opened the rolls of golden book,ah!
Were full of my name.
It's above that sun,,ah!
Have already had my volumes of poetry

I don't know if it's today
Write down these words

Or hundreds of millions of years ago
Had already written them.

I don't know if I am today,ah!
Or in the distant future.
Maybe those golden books,ah!
were enshrined in the future golden hall.

The time of miraculous change,ah!
You incarnated into everything.
The mysterious and distant prehistory
is maybe the human future.

The leisurely change of the universe,ah!
Is maybe the phantom of the mirror
That bright mirror,ah!
is exactly the divine eternity.

Time and time, ah!
Is maybe just you and me
When we disappear
Everything will be vanished without a trace.

III.
I saw the lines of words
shining in the palace of the sun,

incarnated into the golden lights
and flew into my chest.

I was infinitely joyful in my heart,ah!
And saw the picture scrolls.
The completely new paradises,ah!
Smilling on the ground of the world.

The transparent and flashing earth,ah!
Like a charming girl,
the colorful gardens,ah!
were her gorgeous dress.

The clear rivers,ah!
The green mountains of jadite.
The blue eyes of the sea,ah!
Shining the charming glow.

The sky was glittering and translucent as the gem.
The soft white clouds,
the cities of light
appeared the beautiful smiling face.

I opened the picture books of time
and saw the giants.
They were flying in the air,   ah !

rode in a huge spaceship.

The shining planets,ah !

took their greetings to them with smiles.
In the vastness of space
they set up the homes

Their magical eyes,ah!
Twinkled with the surprising wisdom.
Each of them was the mountainous figure and athletic
revealed the extraordinary temperament.

Their quiet eyes
it seemed to have insight into the future.
Everyone was chivalrous,ah!
And filled with holy love.

I looked at the picture scrolls,ah!
As if I had felled asleep
also as if to return to the past
the time of hundreds of millions of years ago.

The golden discs of time,ah!
You spined the wonderful music.
All the future of mankind,ah!

Were stored worshipfully in your chest.

The new giants will appear
in the changing space leisurely.
Let the holy civilization,ah!
To bloom again in the space.

The gates of crystal
leading to different time-space.
Every space of light,ah!
has the rounds of the sun.

The sacred fires of the sun,ah!
Will turn into the gold of the time,
and built the palaces of civilization
in the future centuries.

The flowers of science and art,ah!
Wiil blossom in the gardens of the world.
The lights of the holy civilization
will be turned into a completely new sun.

The huge flowers of the universe
will be the human homes.
That stars of the time
will be turned into sweet wine

Akanksha Agarwal is a multifaceted artist—a poet, dancer, singer, painter, musician and a home- maker par excellence. She gleefully embraces the diverse experiences and perspectives of life and pours it out in her creative pursuits.They spread an aura of happiness and love. Akanksha writes from her heart, dreams with her heart, and being a people's person, lives with her heart.

1. UNTITLED

The dragon in our lives
You are the most haunted animal
That has enveloped our lives
like a blanket of enemy in our body

We as humans are hijacked by this foe
We are at war with this Contagion

We need to wear the shield of happiness and love
To fight with this arrogant and non degradable creature

It's is destroying the bond of humans with nature
The most scariest movie I've ever seen in my life

When a glance in the eye of a doctor
Your image becomes blurred
The sailors of our life
The god of humans

Let's join our hands together
Fight with this invisible human
And let your home be your best friend !

2. ILLICIT EMOTIONS

The Spider and The Cobweb on the ceiling ,the man in her life,
Staring at the insect , for her survival,

Her eyes couldn't blink watching her new friend,
Her day would pass murmuring to the insect,

Love like Termite was feeding her Heart,
She was smiling with sparkling eyelids after long,

Like band of colours portraying different emotion,
She was becoming frail and weak,

She cried out, to pronounce her anguish,
Her lips from ages were summoned to pin drop silence,

He was the last resort for this quadriplegic frame,
His hissing sound ,was the most soothing lyrics ,to die in peace!

3. UNTITLED

While strolling in the beautiful meadow,
 His grip was like a bouquet clasping her hand,

The silence was overpowering , gossiping about their love,
It could brew coffee and Baked crossbones,

The footsteps were the signs of their bond snowballing,
The silent smile was like a sunflower blooming their hearts,

The vineyards around them were intervening   like drugs in
their body,
Their eyelids appearing sedative and slumberous,

The sunset was bridging them closer,
Acting as a catalyst with smoldering feelings,

As the darkness was promising to ignite their emotions,
Their cravings were unfurling as poison!

4. UNTITLED

The blood oozing from
the flesh are my tears.
Tears want to portray
my hunger for you,
you being my soulmate.
Soulmates are never apart,
apart from people who
are jealous and obnoxious.

The seasoning of your
love savours me perfect,

perfect while walking
down the aisle with
you ever,
ever would I want to
vacate your heart,

hearts get gratified
when emotions compile
each other's arms,
arms around each other
trigger the intimacy
forever and ever!

5. UNTITLED

She, the personification of a lioness ,
Ferocious and sharp edged for her duties,

Her hands in gloves and blood have been my soother,
The most courageous metal,

Her Robotic brain ,unwavering her performance,
Patients comfort, drives high spirits and pleasure in veins,

Her work place , the Temple of the house,
The seat she cherishes the most,

The most Fearless women on the globe,
With clock running not faster than her fingers,

The sunset just an indication,
Bones declining as inchmeal,

My tears like every drop of her love ,
showering her blessings on my cheeks,

Her hairy ,rough and itchy forehands,
 The glass of impressions, hard work , sincerity and devotion!

Such journeys are endless and selfless ,
Like fire in the forest, igniting like a Goddess!

Cheri Woods has been a resident of Hawaii for over forty years enjoying the richness of teaching and learning along with her students. Her career included training teachers in a literacy program for Hawaiian students, as well as years of her own classroom teaching. She loved weaving reading and writers' workshops into the curriculum. Cheri also taught students in Portugal and Canada. Upon retirement, she enjoyed teaching literacy in the Women's Correctional Center and writing a children's book. Now she writes prose, poetry and articles for her retirement center's newsletter. At the age of twenty-seven, Cheri lost her mother to cancer. Having lost the love of his life, Cheri's father never remarried. She and her dad became best friends, and it has been her greatest joy to write 'TIL THEN OUR WRITTEN LOVE WILL HAVE TO DO (Aignos 2000) a compilation of his love letters. Although her name is on the cover, she considers him the true author.

ROMANCING THE CLAY

Wheel starts spinning, gathering speed
clay wedged and ready,
my hands encircle and begin to press,
seeking centering and a new creation.

Soon it wobbles, then wobbles hopelessly
and I must surrender my expectations once again.
Discouragement reigns
between my last joyful experiences and now.

My old potter's wheel and I danced together
until it got damaged and deemed unfixable.
Its passing left a gap in time
that has taken a toll on my confidence.

With a new one, I muster up hope
to try again…and again.
A friend came to offer advice,
"don't worry if it isn't perfect."

Not sure that "perfect" is even what I seek anymore.
So, I keep trying, and have a few uncentered, imperfect pieces
to fire.
I have not mastered the clay,
its stronger will prevailing.

As I work, thinking of God as the Master Potter
and me as his clay, I wonder.
Is He frustrated when I won't allow His shaping hands near me
or, when I refuse to center, or let my will defeat His perfect
plans for me?

So, now I am again clay covered and discouraged, but not giv-
ing up,
because, I know a very patient potter who never gives up on
me,
declaring lovingly with no hesitation
that I am His most perfect Masterpiece.

RENTALS

Car rental lot, busy with traffic, as newly washed ones,
dripping and shiny pull in, and soon disappear with a new dri-
ver.
Dirty ones take their place, as drivers exit, vacation over,
leaving their trash and filth behind, without a second glance.

With invisible owner, these rentals are treated poorly and dri-
ven roughly,
soon to be replaced with newer models, for the ever-demand-
ing vacationers.

Handlers hustle to quickly replenish vacancies.
Time is money, and a quick turn-over is everything.

Similar to this place, a much different one also rents to thrill seekers.
Their models, once child-like and pure are quickly rented out and turned over again.
Users here, also dish out rough treatment, leaving their filth and scorn behind.
Oftentimes with bruises, blood, broken bones, and forever crushed spirits.

With fresh clothes and makeup, comes the quick turn-around.
Time is money.
The terror and despair of trafficking is covered over with drugs and caked on lipstick.
Hopeless numbness, resignation, slavery. Used models discarded, and replaced
with an endless new supply.
The monster must always be fed; lust and greed are never satisfied.

LINGERING IN GRATTITUDE

Gratitude, I think is the lubricant of the parched soul
the ambrosia of the hungry spirit

the well-spring for a weary heart.

With retirement comes more time for reflection,
and development of the new habit
of putting on those forgotten "rose-colored" glasses
left dusty on the shelf of a busy life.

In pausing to consider the past,
gratitude is the response to the outcomes of
those life-changing events,
huge challenges and heart-wrenching decisions.

For God's angels appearing,
just when I needed wisdom and burdens lifted.
For the roads not taken, and the ones taken
all leading me to here, to now.

Sometimes on evening walks with my puppy,
gratitude for God's provision overwhelms.
I linger as the rising silhouette of the moon
peeks through clouds, and finds me.

MATTOLE MORNING

With morning gatherings completed, we go inside, and quiet
settles over the garden again.

Bathed in midmorning sun, the rusty old gate swings lazily from the string latch.

Pink cosmos dance with dill in the gentle breezes as white butterflies flutter among them.

Tiny sow bug tanks uncurl and set off to resume their bountiful garden feasts.

Purple profusions of petunias and pansies line the fence supported by rustic bark posts.

Pussy Galore, the feline queen, stalks silently on a secret mission to another part of the yard.

Dropped carelessly, the rusty old rake lies near the purple eggplants, shiny and thriving, brought to fruition by the summer sun.

The white speckled hen, clucking nervously, seeks an escape for her brood through the fence.

Chased out for the second time that morning, she now flutters up to the top, leaving her secret entrance still a mystery.

With Pussy Galore not far behind, the last chick peeps frantically as it races up and down the fence line.

Eventually, it finds the tiny hole and rejoins the brave, little band, seeking new shelter from ever present danger.

In the distance, sounds the piercing cry of the circling hawk.

A Mattole morning begins.

TURNING 70 WITH WATER LILIES

"It's easy," says my teacher.
"Just use this color first with lots of water."

I stare doubtfully at her picture of water pads and lilies.
"Impossible," my brain screams,
as I examine her serene pond with its purple shadowing
lifting up the floating objects while hinting at depths below. \

She continues, "Use cool color here and warm color here."

"But I'm turning 70, I can't possibly do this," I think.

The lesson proceeds,"Use this masking liquid to save the white spaces, and then swirl the water like this."

As I am mesmerized by the magic flowing from her brush and her positive instructions; my mind begins to imagine a slight possibility and I mutter, "well, I can try."

Turning 70 is starting to seem more like new beginnings now, rather than so many endings. Sure, there were big endings like retirement, and moving and an identity change. But those changes have only ushered in time for a new richness of friends, involvements and creativity.

As I breathe in sweet gratitude for so many blessings, proceed with my life into a new decade of rich possibilities and yes, water lilies.

Daniel S. Janik is a retired physician and an educator, naturalist, actor, DanceSport enthusiast, artist, poet, author, publisher/producer and vocal advocate of transformative learning in all its various forms. He is the author of over sixty books and publications including the multi-award winning book "Unlock the Genius Within (Rowman and Littlefield Education 2005). His published works cross numerous genres under a variety of pen names. Single-author poetry book publications include FOOTPRINTS, SMILES AND LITTLE WHITE LIES (Savant 2008), THE ILLUSTRATED MIDDLE EARTH (Savant 2008), and LAST AND FINAL HARVEST (Savant 2008). He has been a contributing poet to the last ten years of Savant Poetry Anthology. His cinematic documentary, "Clean Water, Common Ground," (Savant Media 2020), received two Telly awards for best documentary. He is currently lead actor in the upcoming made-for-television movie, "Static," scheduled to air in mid-September 2021.

HANU O PELE

Morning murmurs,
Breath of Pele,
cool
curious
confidant
caressing

Midday trades,
Pele's touch
hot
heavy
hopeful
hedonistic

Evening Waves
Pele's thoughts,
distant
deep
dark
desirous

Midnight Stars
Pele's whispers,
soft
sighing
soporific.

Ellen Rückmann-Bruch is a sixth-grade student at St. Andrew's Priory in Honolulu. In 2020, she began writing a series of poems reflecting on life during the COVID-19 pandemic and the beauty and inspiration we can find in the world around us even during difficult times. Ellen's work has appeared in Honolulu Civil Beat.

BRIDGES

I.

If I were a bridge
I would be a sure pathway
for people to find each other,
to discover how they connect
in a world where bridges
sometimes fall short
with people wanting to cross them
but not knowing what to expect.

II.

If there were no bridges
where would we be?
Perhaps alone and afraid,
left in the dark,
wanting to hide,
unable to see through
to the other side.

HEARTACHE HAIR SALON

During the pandemic I imagine
I am the owner of the Heartache Hair Salon.
I make wigs for people whose hair
comes out and stops growing

when they are ill. They no longer
want to move or show themselves
because they fear their friends may leave.
My wigs put them at ease,
soothe their heartache,
help them forget their pain.

Robert Uhene Maikai, Editor

Rüdiger Herzing Rückmann has written poetry most of his life, and studied under Tess Gallagher and Hayden Carruth. He is Director of Advancement at Hawaii Youth Symphony. His poems have appeared in ALOHA LA'A KEA (2020 Savant Poetry Anthology) and in galleries and exhibitions, including the Albright-Knox Art Gallery in Buffalo, New York. He is the author of "Offering" in Friends Journal. His essays have been featured in the Honolulu MidWeek's "Chasing the Light" column.

SALLY'S SIREN SONG

My neighbor Sally comes home from long shifts
of standing for hours sorting other people's groceries
and miseries at checkout during a pandemic,
withstanding their fits as they run short of money.
She holds her ground on legs as tired as stone,
a woman who has worked decades to make
her wandering husband feel like a king
in their small apartment where they sleep
in separate bedrooms and she pays the rent.

She arrives home spent but spirited, knowing wine
will soothe her for hours on end as she releases
gentle contempt for women and men who only see her
as an aging clerk, her hair unkempt, a little too red
to hide the gray, but then her voice grows more insistent
with her husband as she rues bargains they have made
to stay together. Neighbors, invited over, hear Sally's siren
song
as she crashes down for the night and they leave quickly,
not wanting to see this couple drown.

TO THE LIMIT

What happens when I'm ninety-five years old
and can no longer speak? When all my bite is gone

and I'm too weak to fight? Do I retreat altogether
and regret that I aimed high, that I always believed
that limits never ended with the sky?
Or do I keep going, knowing inside I may
be rediscovered like a hero who lost his way?

WISTERIA

New wisteria reaches pell-mell beyond
my porch, seducers spreading lilac hope.
Their vines spread as they push away spines
of gentler plants that cower in retreat.

Young children roam in late afternoon,
before mothers and fathers call out
to make sure they safely come home
as evening dominates a fading sun.

Robert Uhene Maikai, Editor

Kaethe Kauffman PhD is a retired Associate Professor of Art, having taught at the University of California Irvine and Chaminade University in Honolulu among others. She innovated inter-disciplinary team-taught courses like "Art and Writing," and "Art and Psychology." A multi-award-winning poet, her poems appear in ALOHA LA'A KEA (2020 Savant Poetry Anthology), ENTWINED (2019 Savant Poetry Anthology), KINDRED (2018 Savant Poetry Anthology), RUNNING FROM THE PACK (2015/16 Savant Poetry Anthology) and VOLUTIONS (2014 Savant Poetry Anthology). She authored the novel LIBIDO TSUNAMI (Savant 2016) by Cate Burns (a pen name).

THE PRIMAL MODERN

In childhood,
When a neighbor pruned foliage,
That evening, a bonfire would blaze.

Smelling smoke,
Everyone followed the floating path,
Grabbing wieners, marshmallows and ukuleles
Along the way.
When dusk fell, the songs began.

To me,
The fire seemed as large as a house.
Faces of all ages glowed orange as we
Ate, joked and sang.
Brave folks imitated Elvis Presley in a dance
At the fire's edge.

Perhaps we looked like an African clan
Whose rhythmic movements held deep meaning.
Although we had no idea what our dancing meant,
A primal camaraderie
Lit us from within.

SNAKE LOVERS

On a desert hike,
I discover
Two six-foot long serpents
Together in a dry stream bed,
Wound around each other,
Resembling the medical staff carried by Hermes.

I feel sudden joy
Pour through me.
With these two bedazzling creatures,
Hermes brings me a message of
Wonder.

I join with
Ancient and indigenous people who
Revere the rebirth
These beings symbolize.
Every two months,
Incredibly, the snakes
Slide free of their old casing
To emerge fresh into the world,
Healed.

A yellowish tan skin with

Interlacing brown diamond shapes adorn the pair
With astonishing beauty.
From six feet away, I look for rattles.
Finding none, I hover close,
Crooning to them.

You are beautiful,
Spectacular.
Thank you for letting me
Sit with you.
What a blessing you give me.

These Bull snakes have no poison.
The entwined pair likely enjoy
Romance.

I stay with them,
My chant of praise ongoing.
All three of us take
The time we need.

After an hour or more,
The two slowly unwind and one moves away,
Out of the arroyo,
Across pebbly sand,
Up a vertical boulder

Along a narrow ledge
And disappears behind it.

Twenty minutes later,
The other snake goes,
Following the exact path
Of its mate,
To the inch.

They've given me a marvel.
I sing my goodbyes.

MEDITATION

My meditation teachers say it's good
To observe my thoughts.
But when I silently listen,
My mind produces

Cruel accusations,
Vampire voices,
Internal scolding,
Jabbering criticisms,
Bad-mouthed trolls,
Insistent insults,

Icky crud,
Hidden cooties,
Lurking falsehoods,
Deep dread,
Malevolent gremlins.

Maybe tomorrow's meditation
Will be better,
Free from the childhood litany.

Then I remember my teachers' advice.
To be mindful and neutral is enough.
With that guidance,
Today's meditation becomes a success.

HURTLING

As a child, I hurtled non-stop,
Fleeing from older siblings,
Scuttling up trees,
Swinging from a knotted rope to drop on a pile of maple
leaves,
Diving into the lake with cold rapture,
Flopping my body onto the ground to roll down long grassy
hills,

Repeating these glories time and again with rushed glee.

Now older, I hold back,
Careful of each step.

Yet I ride on airplanes, thrust through space at horrifying speeds.
Occasionally I speak to groups, exposing thoughts with mental velocity.
I exhibit artwork, a creative race toward a stress-filled deadline.
I sing in a choir where I spill ecstasy into the air around me.

I haven't lost spirit,
I've found new rambunctious joys.

DEAD GIRL'S FLOAT

One day,
Aged nine,
Swimming alone as usual,
I decided to breast-stroke across the neighborhood lake,
About one-half mile.

Midway in the watery expanse,

I could barely see the other side.
An odd feeling engulfed me,
Weariness at my core.
I couldn't go on.
For the first time in my young life,
I'd pushed too far.

My stomach flip-flopped
While small electric pangs of fear
Zapped around it.

In later years, as an adult,
I forced myself
Through discomfort,
Surged beyond panic,
Ignored illness,
Until collapse
Landed me in a hospital.

At nine,
I knew better.
I rotated onto my back,
Arms outstretched
In complete surrender,
The Dead Man's Float.

I gazed at a low gray sky,
That comforted me,
Until I felt miraculous strength
Flow once more.

I reset my course
For the far shore.

Robert Uhene Maikai, Editor

Cigeng Zhang from China is a freelance translator. Her several poems were included in the Savant poetry anthologies of SHADOW AND LIGHT (2017 Savant Poetry Anthology), KINDRED (2018 Savant Poetry Anthology), ENTWINED (2019 Savant Poetry Anthology) and ALOHA LA'A KEA (2020 Savant Poetry Anthology). Her bilingual poetry collection, ROUGE IN THE WATER, was published in China in 2017. In addition her poems have appeared in the UK in the LOST TOWER anthologies (2014-2017) and in POETIC BOND III, IV, V, VI, VII, VIII, IX and X (2013-2020), UK

LEMONADE CUP

The moon gives me a cup of peace

I want to share it with you

Is your rooftop open

Night talks lingering

Who will drink a toast

and make a cross-cupped fond kiss

MAGPIE IN WINTER

The full winged magpie

flitted about

in front of my window

several times

Greyish white circles

skimmed over fast

I felt the happy quiver

of the bird

Do you carry a greyish white luck?

What is it?—I asked the happy bird

Oh, I'm sending a snow to the moon

That's it – The bird twittered

But who has ever seen
this phenomenon happen?
Please tell me, my lucky bird
But the bird soon disappeared

ADAGIO

the brook
pebbles scattered
like stone flowers

I took off my shoes
barefoot treaded lightly
on the flowers

feet slippery as fish
sliding over the smooth petals
a lithe dance of grace

the shallow stream
murmuring past thru
a soft adagio in a flow

Robert Uhene Maikai, Editor

V. Bright Saigal is an India-born American writer, poet, novelist, screenwriter and film Director/Producer, he currently works as a Creative-Consultant while fundraising for Hollywood film projects.

His poems appear in SHADOW AND LIGHT (2017 Savant Poetry Anthology), ENTWINED (2019 Savant Poetry Anthology) and FIRST BREATH (2010 Savant Poetry Anthology), the first of Savant's annual poetry anthologies.

TEARING HEART

High tide of sorrow surging in my heart

Searching for the list moments once woke up tipples of sweet memories

Your smile, your voice and your countenance still remain in my heart like a rainbow

Under the evil smile I hide those wounded sutters on my heart

Once those moments you shared lostfar behind the horizon somewhere

Tearing my heart you left me, and nested somewhere behind the sky

Sailing with the nimbus sitting in a dream boat

Leaving be behind you sailed far from the earth and live beyond somewhere

Those sweet moments once you gave me still blowing g in life

Like a tender wund hugging the ripples in the lake

Once thse memories swung like a tender leaves in the garden

Your smile, you voice and the melodies of your songs went

Silent in the dance hall and in my heart for ever

Leaving me behind, you vanished like cuckoo

From the middle of the jungle and you went silent

The ripples in my heart stood still and waited for you laughter shins

But didn't come even once and my soning heart longing for you, hear

Come once again and adore my love,

Take me to your world, far from this earth, let me rejoice again

Those old melodies are the rhythm in.mu heart and I miss for ever

Come once and and wake up those jingles once laughed dancing

MELODY OF LOST LOVE

Rising in my heart the high tide of sorrow

And, hear afar those jingles of laughter again

Once I forgotten, now surging from the depth

Once in my life you bested and filled fragrance

The spring arrived, so did the cuckoo signing love melodies

Plodded at the shore of lake holding hands we walked

One dawn arrived, waving wings in the sky, and filled happiness

Love blossomed, and arrived the birds and butterflies filling my garden

In my heart filled you the spring and the songs of love

As the sun sunk, liking the water at the end of horizon

Arrived darkness swallowing the day, winking the stars woke up in the sky

Breaking my fort, arrived the palanquin of destiny, grabbing it flew upon the sky

Leaving me behind, tearing my heart, dobing my heart now bleeding for Kong

The lamp in my life lit up for ever, as the blowing wing playedyhe song of forlorn

Swelling at the bosom, I welled the waves hitting the four walls of my heart

Leaving me alone you vanished, and your laughter stllechoing in my heart

Flooding sorrow taking me away from the blossomed garden of happiness once I lived

Come once again and adore those memories of the moments we shared once

And, let medubmerge under ashes in my pyre, leaving behind the memories of those old days.

RHYTHM OF JINGLES

From the depth of my heart still hearing the rhythm of your jingles

Waking up those old melody you sang once

The ripples of happiness pampering the shores of my heart and

Swinging in my garden a tender leaf when the evening wind woke up hertpuchning

Tenderly feeling still coming up and lisding those memories

Of your melifious voice and moonlit countenance

Once lit my life in love and tenderly touch you gave

Not leaving from the meadow of my memories

I may perish with the test of time on the anvil of life
When the whack of destiny crush me mercilessly
And, weeping my heart, yearn to earn your love again
But, leaving this world and me you vanished
Your laughter, your countenance and your tender feelings
Still knocking at my door, waking me up and I weep
Love perennial and the lovers are sailors on life
A small wind may turn them up down and let them sink in the sorrow
Love is fragrant and shows SEED of trust on the heart
Love turns a man , man, without love where light in the human heart
Love will prevail even if we parody and disappear under the ashes in a pure
The love will remain in our heart even when we vanish from this world
Come once again and adire me, let me fall in love shown even in my next birth
Only you I will love, even if I reborn a hundred birth...
Come ooncce again and live me...

TALES OF LAUGHTER

Sitting in a tree in my garden weeping thr cuckoo
For want of his lost lover somewhere he lost once
Like in my heart, swelling the broken heart bleeding

Your memories needling once again after the evening

When the sun lick   the lilac and painting the horizon once again

My heart sunk shims seeing glittering stars winking at me laughing

Once we walked along the shore of this lake dreaming

And, told many tales and laughter at each other

Your laughter and itsechoe still remains on my heart somewhere

More often surge like a high tidreafyeta long dull moments

Your laughter, your jingles and your memories

Still floeing somewhere st the bosom in my heart

Your song wok upa million dreams I'm my heart

And your melodies woven a billion colors in hope

Once I lost all in the test of time when the dedtinstolen you from my life

And you nested far away in the heaven, sailing the life pondering the

Naughty nimbus and cloud across the sky,

The stars and the moon you made cohorts

Leaving behind me you left my world tearing my heart

Come once again and at least grow as rose in my garden

Or hatch from a nest near in the tree the Robin lives

Your smile, and the shy you hide under the veil still I remember

The crescent in the sky slowly ascending touching the mountain top

There you may live as a swan or in the lake at the valley

You may reborn ad the lotus smiling at hhr dun

Wherever you rise, call me there, leaving this sorrow I will

Come hug you and live around till the bell rings to take me to

The world you bested now, where I will knock at the door

And, unveil the story you told once.

Come once again and adore me.

GALLOP OF WILD HORSES

Far in the east rising the reddish sun

Smiling at the meadow slepping under the fur of mist

Hearing gallop of the wild horses running to grass in the jungle

Wearing the red apron the sun again climbing to the slope of the horizon

Wearing the brown and black flying across the sky are the dove and crows

Searching a piece of guava reached the parakeet in my garden

Ripen and fallen lying the red and yellow fruits all over

Touching the shore the ripples kissing and retreat laughing

Still in my heart you prevail and love like the moon in the sky

Well lit my heart once you nested there and lived

Inviting the spring you made turned my life a festive

Once I woke up from the ash filling surprise seeing you re-
joiced

The aspiring and the autumn gone , arrived winter in cold and
misty

Fast and ferocious blew the wind, turned a tornado

And, you left me one morning sleeping silently

You never smiled again, your laughter my heart yearned to
hear

I wept, and sunk in sorrow and buried under the shadow once
again

Tearing my heart you left silent and morose,

Playing the string of forlorn songs I sunk, my heart melt down

Never again heard I your melodies except in my dreams once
you sang

Will I hear your voice, will I see you face and those moonlit
vibrance?

Longing my heart once again waiting to adore you again

Where in the corner of the darkness you hid, there will come
in

A chariot and ride you till the last gate of this universe

Lit a lamp in.my.life again and wake those laughter fied down
once

Come again, come once and wake up the brook in my heart

He lost somewhere and died down once you left

Bring those full moon and the stars into.my life and make

A garden like the one in the sky dear.

Born on November 16, 1936, award-winning poet **Bhupesh Chandra Karmakar** spent his tenure with the Indian Air Force, traveling vastly about India and various countries like Singapore, Dubai, UK and USA. He started writing about his vision of mystical life in various articles and stories in English after interacting with people and sharing their experiences. His published books include DESERTED BIRDS (New Delhi Publishers 2017), BLISS IN ISLAND LIFE (Cyberwit.net 2017), A BLOSSOMED FLOWER (BlueRose 2016), ILLUSION OF FRIENDSHIP (BlueRose 2016), FOCUS ON ILLUSORY GOSSIP (BlueRose 2016), BLISS IN DREAM (Cyberwit.net 2016), A BUNCH OF FLOWERS (Cyberwit.net 2016), A GARDEN OF SWEET SMELLING FLOWERS (BlueRose 2016), GENERAL KNOWLEDGE (BlueRose 2016), THE DROPS OF DEW (PartridgeIndia 2015), THE PAIR OF PIGEONS (Quills Ink 2014) and BLISS OF EMIGRATIONAL LIFE (Dasgupta & Company, 2004/5).

CHILDHOOD MEMORIES

When I was a small child,
I used to go outside to play
around our courtyard
with my friends.
We had a habit of running around
the yard and jumping. We used
to play games with
other children.
I would try very hard to catch
the huge balloons that would
float above us.
As a child, I was encouraged
to play in ground, which
was surrounded by
natural beauty.
When we were sweating from the sun's
Heat, we ran to the nearby lake in
the village to cool down.
Every evening, the children used
to meet collectively to chatter
and exchange stories about their day.
Their voices still echo in my
mind, as if it was dream but
things changed when I grew.
I used to feel charming and used

to smile all the time in
the delighted evening.
Childhood may be considered as
happiest period, but it might not be
happy for everyone.
My village was full of children who
used to laugh and play, but that
changed when the child grew.
The happiness of my childhood has
disappeared and has been replaced
by loneliness, which often
leaves me wondering about it

Robert Uhene Maikai, Editor

Lori Fisher lives and writes on Maui. She received an MA in Writing at the University of Iowa, where she also attended the Translation Workshop. Best known for her translations of the award-winning German poet Reiner Kunze, she also continues to create her own verse. Her poems have appeared in Blueline Magazine, Greene County Council on the Arts Supplement, Civil Beat.

THE INCIDENTALS

The couple coffee in hand with the
black puppy straining at the leash
we pass, nodding, on the beach each morning
or we did
The strawberry blonde boy who bags groceries
usually not mine, but I see him to the left or right
fiddling with the bags waiting for the butter lemons chips and
mayo to reach him
now we pack our own, careful not to touch the conveyer
The pony-tail man riding the bike gripping his red-and-white
surf board
The two cops leaning against the planter wall outside the cof-
fee roaster
always before 11 never in a hurry
The tall thin-legged crossing guard at the elementary school
who grins and stops traffic for gray-haired kids too
The waiter at our brunch place, isn't he too young to work,
why did I not ask his name
The white T-shirt guy who hawks fresh fish from his truck on
the weekend
The Fed Ex gal with pink shoelaces hopping out of her truck
The rubbish driver I only see his suntanned elbow
The woman at the Post Office, bank, fish counter, making keys
at Lowe's, at the Walmart register, sitting on the bench with

her shave ice, handing me bread at the bakery, selling photos at a kiosk, before me at the hairdresser

The man fishing at the park, delivering pallets on a handcart, painting lines on the highway, trimming trees in the median, singing on his skateboard, slicing ham at the deli, begging with upturned hand and soft voice for my takeout or just a dollar

Where are they now
I know where friends family neighbors colleagues are
those I can name
But I am missing
those I didn't realize I had noticed
the connectors between chores and conversations and destinations
Without them the day is colorless and silent, a string of nouns with no adjectives
A puzzle with gaps around each piece, distorting the image
A life without the lives that make it whole
I miss them though I do not know their names

PANDEMIC PARADISE

It's an oxymoron
let's make that clear
and yet

The pandemic is a glimpse into paradise
as it was
as it could be?

The pandemic has brought us
ribbons of shore stretching as far as I see
No beach umbrellas no clusters of crowds just sand and sea

Water so clear I could map out the reef from the shore
outlined like an azure jewel undulating below the waves

Fish jostle in the surge, gathering in schools too many to count
looking back at me I swear not backing away from newly re-
acquired turf
Turtles soar upward toward the surface wings out elegant in
their shells
not caring that I drift with them letting the current carry me in
parallel flight

A whole day on the ridge trail and not a body to be seen
but vistas of shimmering ocean hugging the coastline below,
tiny ripples of surf
like a movie playing in miniature from the peak, just for me

The park, it has parking!

Visitor Center deserted
From the Scenic Outlook you can see the scene
The highway takes us uninterrupted from home to wherever
we want to go
whenever we want to go

We stand at the water's edge at sunset
mesmerized by the neighbor island silhouette
and the melody of waves
No conversation no boom box no Pandora just beauty against
a mango sky

We've got this island to ourselves for just this moment of time
an aberration in the forward march
One moment where the haze of humanity clears to reveal
possibilities past

This island, its beauty radiantly oblivious to the suffering and
grief
but radiant all the same
Glowing growing shining shimmering translucent and lush
silent yet symphonic
So we try to memorize each wave
to greet each fish
to honor each grain of sand
until time moves forward again

Our pandemic paradise a memory or a dream

TO LAUGH

So many ways to talk
We chat text zoom phone email
hours a day
How are you - are you doing ok - let's stay in touch
our new profession communication
We've adapted, we've built a rhythm to the days
I wake up with a list of who to call
Four weeks five weeks six
But today three women meet at the beach
scurrying across to plunge into the sea
Bobbing as we see each others'
eyes blinking hair blowing hands splashing
not frozen on a screen or blurred in pixels
ten feet away but gloriously live
Snorkels askew we tread in place
And we blurt out stories, talking three at once and not wanting
to stop
giddy with the sight of each other
And we laugh
out loud
long giggly exuberant
as we have not in 40 days

Jessie Dunn

TREASURE OF TIME

Infinite love,
moment-by-moment lost in time

Each everyday
souls melt to fashion a heart

Expotentionally, don't be in
go out instead but stay to where you should be

Regardless the circumstances
Regardless of the brightening of a light to a pathway

No trepidations only the courage and love
keeping within the heart a fierce burning

Intense love
given in perfect glowing radiance

It's the load to carry when times gets crazy,
amazingly enduring when life gets heavy .

But a testimony of love,
an anointment of life

Filling in the bumps and bruises

of life's journey

Every moment piled desperately onto the next
stretching forth, reaching out

Its a voyage towards the end-light
in the victory glare

Never a life that can't be restored
a diamond amongst treasures of creation

Knowing how living abundantly,
Bliss with no damper

Life-possession through full sensation;
life complete, a free spirit

Do such in awe
as a blossoming flower

With the fragrance of restoration
Enhancing every moment.

to my dad and mom in appreciation for their love and care

Robert Uhene Maikai, Editor

Loretta Makai

PRESS SAVE

Examine, knowing its all too surreal

Understand when it's all put together

Done

To get the best deal.

COMPLETE IN CAUSE

It's the moment to gain
the time for pain

A life of learning
all in the now,
without being burned

Focus on the horizon
all experience to make
the best possible version

Meditate in the present,
Satisfied to never go back

Stay reminded

to bare matters
all matters of care

Exercise occasionally
to keep well each day

Stay fit:
As time moves on, it plays a factor
It's all about the perspective of the benefactor

Express thoughts through love
For that's how imagination turns to reality

- to my grandchildren and Ohana far and wide

Robert Uhene Maikai, Editor

Ken Rasti

LANIKAI RAIN

I quiet my mind
To be still with you
Alone on my way home
My sweet Lanikai Rain

Like a supersaturated cloud
You shower peace into the pool of my mind
Infinite storms of beauty

I am in uncharted waters
Can I say no?
Should I say no?
But the Queen of all Seas is with me
The King of all Storms is with me

I heard your purple Kili noe Rain tears
Drum lightly on a crimson pane
Just the same

Softly whisper your presence
Are you seeking entrance?
Walk with me
Remain in me
Dance with me
In secret ballrooms

Pua La'a Kea -- Sacred Light of Flower

In ancient Hawai'ian caves

You're the expression of eternal thought in time
My sweet Lanikai Rain
You're an ancient alchemist
Turn my tears into rain

You've created abundant life
You're the ultimate mystic
I want to remain in you
My sweet Lanikai Rain

Rain down on me
Put your spell on me
Rain your love on my heart
My heart has been in draught
My heart needs your ocean
Ocean of love

I am stuck inside your fire clouds
Let your glowing river run through my soul
Let your mysterious sand clouds play in your turquoise ocean
My sweet Lanikai Rain

I heard you never hold back your sweet tears
You rained into my eyes

And the sun came out
My sweet Lanikai rain

Are you cold, Nāulu Rain?
Hold my hands
My hands are a pot of gold
Let my hands do the soothing
Let my hands do the moving

Every time I see you falling
I get down on my knees and pray
There is so much left to say

You gave birth to a field of eternity
A field of dreams
Dreams of you
Dreams of me

As Mother Sky greets each newborn morning
A fresh sweet dew still is given
... Oh, your sweet jealous sky
She misses my Lanikai rain

As I breathe in each newborn morning
So are my thoughts again awakening
I feel closer to you and heaven

Pua La'a Kea -- Sacred Light of Flower

My sweet Lanikai Rain

When a boat comes ashore
The sea has spoken
Sail on home to your underwater cave
Dance with me
In secret ballrooms
In ancient Hawai'ian caves

Here comes the sun
Oh, Such a sweet song
The Sun is cold
The Rain is hot

Home
Home and dry
Home is the temple of your heart
I am home and dry
With you, my sweet Lanikai Rain

I quiet my mind
To be still with you
Alone on my way home
My sweet Lanikai Rain

PRINCESS KA'IULANI

Her heart is on fire
Her heart is the house of prayer
Come out of the dark clouds
Ride the blue moon
Ride the dance of light
In the dark of the night

Her eyes are on fire
Burning with passion
Her eyes talk story
Story of a thousand mystics
Her eyes are the long time sun
Her passion
Oh, Such a sweet incantation
A mystical trance

Where's your home,
Sweet Princess?
Be at home with the Now,
Find your home in the Now,
In our Sweet Hawai'i
A return journey
Coming home to ourselves
In our Sweet Hawai'i

In her eyes
I see the doorway to a thousand journeys
A king without a castle
A queen without a throne
Eternal devotion
To her emotion

Lost in her sweet ocean
Ocean of love
Our Sweet Princess Ka'iulani
Some other place
Some other time
She reached out for the secret too soon
She reached out for the moon

Something in the air tonight
If the stars are right
It's gonna be her turn tonight
Eagles flew out of the night
Her sacred premonition
Feels just right

Oh, Sweet Princess Ka'iulani
See love through her dark eyes
Her Lei of love
Can chase the clouds away

Can find the way
Shine the old lantern
See love through the dark night
Let your vision light up the night

A universal suffrage through the night
See love through the dark clouds
Shine the old lantern
The Kanaka now can see your light

Princess Ka'iulani
I hear your drum beat echo in the night
I hear your ancient melody
Your sweet Hawai'i

Oh, Sweet Princess Ka'iulani
You never left my heart
You never faded away
Come out of the dark clouds
Ride the blue moon
Ride the dance of light

SWEET HOME WAIMANALO

Hello, Hello, Hello
Welcome Home to Mama Nalo

Your big waves of sound space
Oh, such a sweet persuasion
Swept away in your wonder
Your big waves softly whisper
I will catch you when you fall
Oh, such a sweet sensation
An intoxicating love vibration
You can make every day an eternal vacation

A distant boat desires your horizon
Cries out for your mysterious island
Your liquid love
You are the eye in the sky
You are the wind and the rain
A crystal mist
A distant boat is coming home to you

Sweet Home Waimanalo
I am coming home to you
I am so into you
All of you
Gazing slowly at your five shades of blue
Hmmm, was that a wink from your Makapu?

Your playful migrating wales

Got me wondering
Is there a rabbit in your island?

Lost in the beauty of your banyan trees
A deep knowing in silence
Searching for legends in every gentle breeze
A sweet resonance
Show me the way home
My Sweet Home Waimanalo
I am coming home to you

I found the silver lining
In your white cotton clouds
For thousand years
I have been searching for heaven
The Promised Land
Nirvana
Ohana
I found heaven in my Sweet Home Waimanalo
Mahalo

Find heaven in your heart
Find heaven in love
Sweet Home Mama Nalo
Your majestic mountains
Welcome me with Aloha

Every ridge talks story of mystics with Aloha
Mahalo Ke Akua
Mountain lullaby
The soothing source
Your silent knowing
You can see everything with the eyes of Aloha
Even when you have fog in your mind
In your liquid mind

She called out
Hello, Hello, Hello
Welcome Home to Mama Nalo
Ahui Ho
Mahalo Ke Akua
Mahalo Nui Loa
My Sweet Home Waimanalo

A BIG BLUE BIRTHDAY BALLOON

Happy birthday to you
Happy birthday to me
Wild and free
Every second we are born
Every second we are free

No book of law

No big judge
No enigma
No dice
No blame
No victim

I want a big blue birthday balloon
A sweet lullaby
Toys
Kisses in the rain
I want to make every day my birthday
I want to be a nowhere man
A merry-go- round

Who are you?
How old are you?
The real you
Where do the children play?
Are they playing in your heart?

No past
No future
No tripping
Time is but a thought in movement
New beginnings
New endings

Time for a Zen pause

Where is Now?
Take me on a journey into the Now
The journey with no distance

Hey, Mr. Time
Happy Birthday to you
Happy Birthday to me
Rain down on me
Is there a reason
For every season?
Tomorrow starts today

I have sunny tales to share
I am a tropical seabird
Fly with me
I am a migrating wale
Swim with me
Wild and free

Shall I wait for the storm to pass?
Or, Shall I learn to dance in the rain?
Kiss me in the rain

I have sunny tales to share

With my big blue birthday balloon
Fly with me
Wild and free

Happy Birthday to you
Happy Birthday to me
Wild and free
How old are you?
The real you
Where do the children play?
Are they playing in your heart?

BREATH, HA!

Take a deep Breath
Hmmm, Ha

Breath is the Source
Breath is Love
Freedom
Patience
Wisdom

Breath is a Teacher
The Healer

Take a deep breath
Hmmm, Ha

Breath is the symphony
The song
The dance
The melody

Breath is Oneness
Aloha
The journey,
With no beginning
With no end
The way home
Mahalos, Ke Akua

Take a deep breath
Hmmm, Ha

Breath is the blessed marriage
The meeting place of all hearts
The mystery
The beginning
The end

Breath is the Spirit

The breeze
Aloha

Take a deep Breath
Hmmm, Ha

Mahalos, Ke Akua

Kanzy Abdelkhalek is a third-generation student who aspires to influence change and beneficial growth.

A BEHAVIORAL STUDY

The sky, ever so swiftly,
blends with the hollow sea

They are of the unknown,
who seem to embrace those who look beyond their discomfort
They swallow those who elude
and resemble those who weep

The sky and the sea echo an entity
One who deludes their observers

For, a body of freedom and a passage of purity
surfaces its interpretation
Yet, its dangers are unknown
and its wonders are to be sought

Does one find comfort in what they do not know of
Or is it of what is deemed endless?

Humanity seeks the endless call and, simultaneously,
avoids the unnatural face of immortality

*To my best friend who always supports me and to my favorite
teacher who always inspires me*

Mike Lau with Granddaughter Kat Rose

EVERLASTING ETERNITY

I'll be waiting for you, my love,
Each and every day of my life.

I'll be waiting for you, my love!

How very special
every moment together.

It's the season to offer our love
to each other in everlasting eternity.

I'll be waiting for you, my love...

Pressing on forward;
Never to rewind or regret

Always moving straight ahead,
For I'll be waiting for you my love,

I'll be waiting for you, my love.

Being one together in love,
Our thoughts engaged in splendid endearment,

Splendid every time with every memory

That bonds our hearts.

Yes , I'n waiting for you, my love!

to all ohana and beautiful wife

Robert Uhene Maikai, Editor

Robert Uhene Maikai

TRANQUILITY ADORATION

Your beauty goes from the hemisphere above and qualifies the gift from the very

breath given which declares how intriguing it all is .For which it occurs the spectacular

wonderment sustained by the gloriously bestowed beauty . Now further delivered to

every beautiful heart desiring to notice the presence seen in all existence.

As such is the beauty coming from the majestic heavens to now brought down

to earth among men wherefore all may take in the abundance of the supplier's hand.

Do give and share all good things , things from the source of the life giving love.

for every heart , is doing its all own distinguishing in the love continually.

So raise up your hands in celebration ! For the beauty is definitely a

taste of the glorious brilliance reigning in tranquility adornment

our beauty is a lovely flower with many waterfalls around as it

representing chandillers of brightly glowing delight . Random glare of a precious smile

radiants like a warmth of confronting comforting spirit in bringing burning of a tremendous blow trembling of love.

As longing for a satisfying presence with the special touch escalating

perks, and an awe awakening of entire being in the nerve cells. Oh how contemplating

upon every moment to savor the occasion in just brushing up near to feel the rage of

boiling blood . Now so at this very moment giving life to the brain cell tissues of sponges messaging to toes, feet of the tingling satisfaction sensation. Thus found only special

features tantalizingly deep down to the cracking bones in lingering on forever in the

taste buds sensations of the eternal sweetness.

Your beauty resonates to the highest heavens , entangle to engulf those

truly knowing all about beauty . So enlightening the hearts of many to impart in the

liveliness of cascading propensity of power illuminating the brightly transfixed

arraignment in rays of sunlight notably warms up the senses on a cold winter night .

So what an assorting supernatural wonderful aspirations to fulfill the gentle

curves of sway entangle to dominate the fine affirmations without any vexations .

Your beauty is delicate thoughts in patterns of everyday re-
wards. As it sacrificially

gives forensic love by the reflecting of the bright shine in life's
morning refreshing

cool splash of moisture giving off an magnetic attractive décor
of an amazing beauty

perpetual love.

Further do go on away in wanting to keep everything about the
treasured

moments directly upon mind memorably , constant more as it
brings closer to the

heart of beauty . Such advancement exhilarating in palpatating
lavish, lushest

enchanting fragrance of all the world's treasures sincerely em-
braced with much

flavorable love .

It's only real to realize the most divine nature from heights above in the

glistering glow of shine by each demonstrating awestruck display of a father's love

to his jewels of prize possessions.

YOUR BEAUTY BY FAR, WHO CAN KNOW?

So by the assorting special arrangement of flowers speaking gladness

do pervades with the inspirations of a gentle touch bringing an awakening to the mind

at ease being settled.

Do an embellishing enchantment saying to the senses, giving in an enhancement

in the entitlement of a meaningful agreement telling how it's great to be alive and life

is truly worth living

Your beauty majestically seen upon all existence does formulate a sacred

sweet smelling aroma . For it gladly capitulates the softening of hearts. As all those

who are awestruck by the endearing moments of a sun settling in the horizon. How

it may engage exposure to a cool snowflake or the cascading chorus of a sparkling

waterfalls by the pleasing passing of an audacious encounter in seeing the gleaming

smile directly towards making. Bowing down in being so thankful in what occasion

being truly admiring such tremendous beauty. Now how overwhelming gives the senses

of a soul bursting open with all gladness. No never again to distract from the thought

of opulent lavishing, adorable precious in truly making the world seem much better story days taken view of a gratifying enhancement from a pleasing presence.

Notwithstanding in surviving each moment in the reflection of every astounding

way. So which gets all choked up calling out for an oxygen mask in staying alive. How

just by showing in showcasing distinguishingly beautiful in amazing clarity reality. Do

now brings the loveliest bright pearl sparkling tenderly in heart . As such turning back in

gazing in the direction of eyes touching in deep warmth as two becoming one.

Your beauty is in the form of many transcending rainbows cascading

down as waterfalls giving delightment of pure satisfaction in the fondest of memories to tell in the captivating beauty. Now bringing an adornment of a twinkle to sparkle

in the eyes.

So does broadcast of how rare beauty given to viewing audience of the ambiance

which is too wonderful in enabling a picture to hold its image . Spectacularly testifying

the obvious on how lightning has struck in making much more radiant in an awestruck

manner especially showcasing no less of a clamoring beauty.

For now so able to be letting go then at an instant once again hidden, Do only

curtails the splendor of transmitting glow ingesting to satisfy the reflecting image of a

gleaming shine. It's the sparkling from the eyes getting the heavens to open up and inhale the tantalizing ecstatic aroma dispensing from the globe of beauty in the fullness

of delightment. Now manifested in the marvelous partaking of the heavens .

Your beauty is a galaxy of the best brightest shining lights on a sweet scenic

viewroma to every living entity wanting to live another day. So it couldn't make any

sense living tomorrow without the simple presence bringing right here, at this very

moment. For right here caring to ask, " What has here come ?". How just too wonderful

and amazing to look upon!

So overwhelming are in such a dream in every fulfillment about all

elegance. No don't never want to awaken from something really quite pleasant. But rather putting into a wonderment of arraying colorful thoughts that radiants all day long.

AN ADMISSION TO ONLOOKERS

Your beauty majestically wonderment of pure delight in the collapsing

anointing arrangement to vibrate streams of signals to the majority of candidates

perpetuating the reflection of notifications to the populace.

Do let the beauty of the constellations be singing delightfully in the eyes.

So tantalizing beauty may being like a furnace burning with love, evidently in the

luster of derailing desire. Thus the captive multitude of thrilling adornment glowing

overwhelming scent which makes stylist figure in an admission to onlookers reflecting

a pure bristle of enchantment .

How the pure elegance of beauty is an atomic design doing a crystallizing

explosion of waves in pleasureable barrage of contributing rhythm portrayed. It is really

how the heavens goes shouting and screaming of the bountiful beauty of remedy? Just

suffice affordable in capturing all the radiance of a sparkling gleaming gem.

So embarks the treasure in brilliance of creation rapped in stymied of silence

in a reverence heart. Becomes opted in body to manifest in itself among the Lion's heart .

No never about giving up the appetite to ravish a resounding love as beauty really direct

in the assortment of colors echoing clusters above the skies showcasing rainbows Its doing a chant igniting the flames of love to entwine the soft spoken melodies unlocking

time and way of the hemisphere as it burns a constant jolt of graceful love in a mixture

of chemical reaction giving off a sonic boom to spurt out the intensified love in near

radius. Do go enticing to make ramshackle an outwardly affection by colliding into

seemingly an magnetic allure of divine composition. Do allowing the heart to flutter

with a fantasy of fashion to float on air as now with an amazing feeling of passion

engaged.

Your beauty is imminently rising to the highest heaven gleeing, shining

majestically .As it compose its wondrous power of the creation to triumphantly display the content of the special array of ever-so-more efferently bountiful candor of glowing

beauty. For its glowing glistering wonder of the influentially real in the rays of beauty

being transparent. But the glowing beauty crystallizing on hemisphere crystal? Do keep

in mind how innocence of beauty so becomes the vastness sur- roundings which telecast

saying how the group of ladies look like a cloud of celestial angels!

This is the palpasating heart reflecting the union of changing lives in specking at

at this very moment the life personally giving an attraction and blessings received in ulti-

mately being the impact leaving upon the earth. For the heav- ens becomes the reason of

attraction in a better way of life. This acknowledging being rip away announcing it's a tryst cultivated by exploiting in customary connecting union as owning things itself.

A blossoming starlight shining beauty on a hilltop as the reflecting light

transmits down the mountain opening eyes and casting upon the heart alive. Such divine

love which spreads comfortably among the sharing seduction of people selectively

giving a gift of radiance to all whom yearns for something more.

Now able to feasts on a deliverance because of transmutable brides intense

love to be such sweet aroma cascading strikingly below to the masses the overwhelm-

ingly astute presence truly lights up a Kingdom with a tear drop falling. So much glowing in eyes sparkling in high esteem made real to a magnificently beautifully, fully

completed dream come true.

A MOMENT TO REMEMBER

So such tranquility serene quiet , very calm and peaceful island
of Molokai . Where its hangout time with my Grandpa , who now is ready to fix up lunch . Did grasp my attention to tell in getting ready coming to table.

Now ready to get lunch together. Well Grandpa says now lets pule, an Hawaiian word meaning prayer Thus from start to ending of prayer listening but not understanding so soon concluding as he saying, "For Thine is the Kingdom , the Power" then all of a sudden boom-bam Grandpa hits the table with fist! For such awakening in a half-conscious state asking Grandpa, "Why did hit the table?" Now had replied instantly because boy God has a lot of power. As looking straight into my little bitty squirming eyes how got really amazed! How well unknowingly in fully understanding statement and what actually happened. But did get stuck with the memory of how Granpa kept smiling at me over and over .

As later looking back on situation the meaning of memory portrayed. So understood the meaning clearly and at a young age put the fear of God in me. How such a major memory taken throughout life Do get flash back at times thinking how my Grandpa kept smiling back on occasion an idea of thought in the moment to awaken a child to a special intriguing sacred love encounter given to a grandson by a treasured cherished light shooting star my dearest Grandfather !

THE BEST PLACES

Akward moment,
mind boggle thinking as a child with thoughts
of how this could be happening?
The purity of the religion
becoming deformed
and deframed
by a crackling of glass
across a picture
of Angels in mid-cover.

Now just in the seasons
of watching movies at Christmas and Easter.
Do got the sensitive affect
with body and the reality of mind.
Remember as a child

getting distressed
and the heaviness upon conscious spirit.
For got disturbed unable
to sleep at night,
in a very bothersome mood.
How just trying to sleep
but profusely sweating in perspiration
all night long .

How at a young age
viewing the cracked glass
then asking a whole lot
of questions to Mother,
pestering on the reason
for this and that to be.
Declare in answering in
explanation given
that it just felled
in causing the crack.
Though still it wasn't
the comforting answer looked for.
Just still so immensely bothered.
Still asking, "Why?"
So being much disturbed
by the continual question
For it caused a struggle in the soul

and mind.
No one could never understand
something sacred
taken to heart
being in an usual occasion.

Now as a child
thinking how such highly esteemed items
being precious saddens
a heart!

Which is about how a vastly unheralded effect
caused damage to an influential child,
becoming dubious in sensitivity
of mind and heart.
Regarding something damaging
made impact feeling
in much disturbed and distracted
in viewing such discord. Do just
thinking consciously in knowing
it's a beautiful symbol, not to be
any disarrangement .

Thus, again, now taken
to an understanding statement
which says, "Blessed

are the little children
and no one can enter in
unless they become
as like a little child
in receiving precious life.

Harvey Hess (1939-2012) was an American poet, librettist, educator, arts critic and theologian. His life and work are associated primarily with the states of Iowa and Hawai'i. Harvey specialized in poetry with meter and rhyme systems, lyrics for musical setting, and Japanese poetic forms. Five books of his poetry have been published, including TH'AUTUMNAL SEQUENCE: SONNETS OF THE FALL (Eight Pound Tiger 2002); SKIPPED STONES: FACES IN TIME (Eight Pound Tiger1994); HAWAI'I LYRICS (Finial, 1985) and ORCHID ART AND THE ORCHID ISLE (Mālama Arts 1982) and LYRIC IMAGES (private publisher 1962).

WHO KNOWS HOW FAR

Who knows how far this scroll and song
Will go to and fro silk-trade's throng
And reach your ears through ice and snow;
For art is slow to move along
Past death's gates to immortal show?

Since orchids are what you must long
For, I have painted one among
The gifts. Silk's golden road must go
Who knows how far?

But thieves are many, greedy, strong,
Despite the power of the T'ang;
Should no note come, then my life's flow
Joined Heaven's River—freed from wrong—
Who knows how far?

A SONNET TAKEN FROM THE DEAD OF WINTER

Thunder, present and past, under the skin
Of our teeth, rattled us till those high keyed
Herders of storms, Snow Geese, freed from the creed
"Freedom is home," sheltered us in their din.

Like them, we knew ourselves as wonder, kin
Who feed on seed, till I found out his breed,
Their faithless northern love and southern need:
Vagrants the Snow Geese shun as saints flee sin.

Now aching echoes shaking back and forth—
True North; due South—clap bolts from bluff to bluff,
Pale as his face when he took wing in flight.
"Geese clamor," he claimed, "for all migrants' worth
Who, unchaste, were not thunderstruck enough
For my flock's faith in true North, black and white."

Robert Uhene Maikai, Editor

Jennifer Cahill is the recipient of a Masters in Administrative Studies from Boston College. She has been a student of The Writers' Studio and Gotham Writers' Workshop. Publications include SOJOURNER (Chapbook) (Pudding House 2010), and "Rise" in STARS IN OUR HEARTS (World Poetry 2011).

IVY VEINS

Sandpaper linen-
embroidery in pallid hands.
Spirit-thin webs of trees:

pristine; honored.
Ashen bones under cotton
sky finger inflamed

sugar-soft feathers.
Snow, tingling, starts to cling.
Immaculate hues.

FOXY NEUTRINO

The psychology of the sun is strange...

The violinist's taupe
strapped sandals, color of beach
sand, burning, slap tiles

with embedded grime, like
the charred plaster walls of a Syrerian
merchant. Anytime...a fear:

bombs dropped, scarring

an isolated biped life.
Morning edges spill

light the tint of egg-
whites commixed with the yolk, brewing
the dream that souses

the intangable
permeation of the air;
imbued rose colors

of birth; or a prom's
carnation, white tinted blue
like the cottony sky

draped over the fringes
of liminal lives cast onto
the arcane stage

of a paralyzed
mortality. A need
of warmth for the flower,

the snug petals that breach
an infernal cut into
the animus in life.

A stygian gash
insufferable like a pompei
brain cooked into glass,

a fossil the tinct
of diabolical eyes. An
appollyn rises

to seize the sun's foxy
neutrino, more easily
snared than bombs.

HALF MAN

A sketch of cimarron
shades: an appollyon emerges,
her spectre arms reach

like the charcoal bones
of the wild, the webbed trees.
Their silhouette absorbed

into the night clasp
the edge of the curved
slice of moon, cocaine

colored and as potent.
For ancient stories are spun
within its orbit.

It is a black and
white rock that once had oceans,
the orb created

by a long ago
planet colliding with Earth.
A diabolical

world pushes against
our mortal microcosm, in which
molded flesh is a cloak

shaped to kill, and shed.
Stripped of this armour, we meld
into death, a viscous

void of the sublime
intense beating, of puissance,
zoetic. Tincture

of a collapsed white

dwarf, the distant plum red throb
that emits heat, burns.

Earthly demon world
nabs; chalk rubbed into pores.
Human colors drown.

OGRE BONES
Trees' jagged branches
catch the sun sinking a moist
hummus color spread

and coating the edges.
Pointed, thrust into seeping
ink of violet cotton,

is the mountain, chalk
colored. It is a beautiful ogre,
deceptively majestic.

It eyes a village
weaving native life.
Spines of which are wild

burnt-colored trees,

the bones of the forest, its
tangy scent sweet to prey

that lure the lion,
whose deep yellow is the hue
of the indian

sunset. The sky is now
an acrylic portrait. A stoked
fire settling, rose imbued.

Ash color ingrained
into stone embraced by ivory
patches, bone-chilling.

The sugar- soft dirt
covered paths collect footprints.
Carved into a life.

HEART BREAK

Wound those buried
with the toothed crack
of sky. A thread

of buttercup cream

tinted silver
rips the alpine

cottony edges.
A biscupid fuse
pushes the cerise

stream through the veins,
its navigation
nourished by

sweet citrus heavens;
wash of Summers:
green leaves, gardens. Lust

flush like a silk shawl
embroidered
with a pearly flame.

The storm lambastes
sunlight colored
windows that cast

an embrace into
our wintered dusk,
beryl tones of which

absorb the shaded
portrait of loss.
Zoetic flags. Drowned.

Robert Uhene Maikai, Editor

Pua La'a Kea -- Sacred Light of Flower

Multi-award-winning poet **Thomas Koron** was born in Grand Rapids, Michigan on May 19, 1977. He has attended Grand Rapids Community College, Aquinas College, Western Michigan University, Northern Illinois University and the American Conservatory of Music. He currently lives within the Chicago metropolitan area. His poems have appeared in ENTWINED (2019 Savant Poetry Anthology), KINDRED (2018 Savant Poetry Anthology), SHADOW AND LIGHT (2017 Savant Poetry Anthology), RUNNING FROM THE PACK (2015/16 Savant Poetry Anthology) and BELL-WETHER MESSAGES (2013 Savant Poetry Anthology).

155

THE CASTLE OF WISDOM UPON THE HILL

The castle of wisdom upon the hill

One hundred and twenty-five years ago

Was founded. And, it continues to still

Inspire those who surround it to know

That they all have future dreams to fulfill.

As young men and women vow their new pledge

To all change their futures for the better—

A river flows near the tall castle's edge.

It still welcomes new students to the pack

As they open an acceptance letter.

Crossing the grounds with books held in a sack,

They continue to make new friends and roam.

Proudly wearing colors of red and black,

They welcome this campus as their new home.

in Commemoration of the Founding of Northern Illinois University

UNDER QUARANTINE

As new cases slowly begin to grow,

A strange disease threatens our existence.

All across the globe, fear begins to flow,

As updates now grip us with persistence.

From public places, people start fleeing,
Unable to enjoy the open air.
Now, we look all around ourselves—seeing
Loneliness, isolation and despair.

Venturing out, we keep a safe distance
To try and protect our own well-being.

Trapped inside, we fight a fearful feeling
That makes us paranoid and insecure.
We all hope that the world will start healing,
As doctors endlessly search for a cure.

A CARDINAL NOW CALLS OUT THROUGH THE TREES

A cardinal now calls out through the trees,
Hoping its lonely presence will be known,
As the branches slowly sway in the breeze.

The bird sings with the hope that one of these
Days it will no longer sing on its own—
A cardinal now calls out through the trees.

Over a grassy field, it flies with ease,
And comes to rest near a creek on a stone;

157

As the branches slowly sway in the breeze.

Up in a nearby elm tree, the bird sees
A mate to keep it from being alone—
A cardinal now calls out through the trees.

The surface of the lakes begin to freeze,
And they wait for their young to be full-grown;
As the branches slowly sway in the breeze.

They watch as the last of their young now flees,
And all their children from the nest have flown.
A cardinal now calls out through the trees,
As the branches slowly sway in the breeze.

WITH THE HOPES THAT OUR PATHS WILL CROSS ONCE MORE

Here I walk alone down a distant shore,

Watching the sunset, as clouds drift away,

With the hopes that our paths will cross once more.

My mind feels empty and my nerves feel sore,

Wishing to meet again some other day,

Here I walk alone down a distant shore.

Recalling how my heart sank to the floor,
Not knowing exactly what I should say,
With the hopes that our paths will cross once more.

You turned away, and then walked out the door,
Even after I had begged you to stay,
Here I walk alone down a distant shore.

I keep walking, my tears begin to pour,
Wondering what sort of price I must pay,
With the hopes that our paths will cross once more.

I remember promises we once swore,
And yet, you are not here with me today.
Here I walk alone down a distant shore,
With the hopes that our paths will cross once more.

EVERY TIME MY THOUGHTS RETURN TO CHILDHOOD

Every time my thoughts return to childhood,
Images of her shimmer through my head.
Thinking back to the days when we both would
Go playing outside after we had read.
Rainy days would keep us inside instead—
Recess was never allowed on wet slides.

As the sun came back out, we soon were led
Outdoors; never leaving each other's sides.
Now, she graces these lines, although she hides
Deep within the structure of this rhyme—
Search for where within these lines she resides;
The answer then will be revealed in time.
And, as the story now comes to an end,
I dedicate this to my childhood friend.

Michael Joseph Masor

.

ISLE OF TREASURE

Friends aboun', all over town.
Aloha, Isle of Treasure.

Waves crash on the beach, rainbows stretch out of reach.
Aloha, Isle of Treasure.

Keiki and turtles play, down around by the bay.
Aloha, Isle of Treasure.

Enjoying the view, from up in Ka'u.
Aloha, Isle of Treasure.

Eating plate lunch in the sun, days in Hawai'i are so fun.
Aloha, Isle of Treasure.

With much love in the air, Hawaiian people will never scare.
Aloha, Isle of Treasure.

Enter hao'le thinking, now watch Hawaiian culture start sinking.
Farewell, Isle of Treasure .

Induce fear of Corona, from Hilo to Kona.
Farewell, Isle of Treasure .

Eliminate hugs, keep a distance. put up zero resistance.
Farewell, Isle of Treasure .

Turn up the dials, by masking up all the smiles,
Farewell, Isle of Treasure.

If you remember, an Island of Splendor,
Eesist at all costs, before all is lost!
Restore ALOHA, Isle of Treasure!

Robert Uhene Maikai, Editor

First Breath - 2010 Savant Anthology of Poems

Zachary M. Oliver (Editor)

72 pp. 5.25" x 8" Softcover

ISBN 978-0-9845552-2-2

Twenty-nine poems by ten outstanding poets and writers selected for their outstanding merit, including Helen Doan, Erin L. George, Jack Howard, Daniel S. Janik, Scott Mastro, Zachary M. Oliver, Francis H. Powell, Gabjirel Ra, V. Bright Saigal and Orest Stocco.

Robert Uhene Maikai, Editor

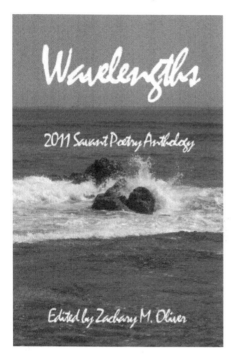

Wavelengths - 2011 Savant Poetry Anthology

Zachary M. Oliver (Editor)

102 pp. 5.25" x 8" Softcover

ISBN 978-0-9829987-6-2

Thirty-eight poems by sixteen outstanding poets and writers including Four Arrows, Penny Lynn Cates, J. R. Coleman, Nadia Cox, Helen Doan, Erin L George, IKO, Daniel S. Janik, Vivekanand Jha, A. K. Kelly, Zachary M. Oliver, Cara Richardson, Michael Shorb, Jason Sturner, Jean Yamasaki Toyama and Jeremy Ussher.

LONDON BOOK FESTIVAL AWARD

Fifty-Eight Stones - 2012 Savant Poetry Anthology

Daniel S. Janik (Editor)

128 pp. 5.25" x 8" Softcover

ISBN 978-0-9852506-5-2

Thirty-four outstanding poems by eleven exceptional and many award-winning poets including Shawn Canon, Nadia Cox, Helen Doan, David Gemmell, Richard Hookway, Daniel S. Janik, Vivekanand Jha, Doc Krinberg, Julie McKinney, Francis Powell and Jean Yamasaki Toyama.

Robert Uhene Maikai, Editor

Bellwether Messages - 2013 Savant Poetry Anthology

Daniel S. Janik (Editor)

134 pp. 5.25" x 8" Softcover

ISBN 978-0-9886640-4-3

Thirty-two selected poems by fourteen outstanding poets including Tender Bastard, Shawn P. Canon, Natascha Hoover, IKO, Daniel S. Janik, Vivekanand Jha, Thomas Koron, Doc Krinberg, Cathal Patrick Little, Peter Mallett, Emma Myles, Ken Rasti, Uhene' and Ashley Vaughan.

LONDON BOOK FESTIVAL AWARD

168

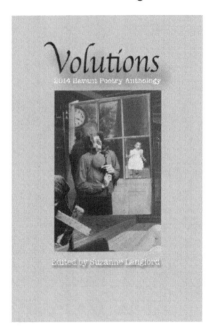

Volutions - 2014 Savant Poetry Anthology

Suzanne Langford (Editor)

146 pp. 5.25" x 8" Softcover Pocketbook ISBN
978-0-9915622-1-3

Thirty-six exceptional poems by fourteen outstanding poets including Noemi Villagrana Barragan, Elsha Bohnert, Hans Brinckmann, Helen R. Davis, K. Lauren de Boer, Duandino, Lonner F. Holden, Daniel S. Janik, Kaethe Kauffman, Suzanne Langford, Lucretia Leong, C. P. Little, Leilani Madison and Lady Mariposa.

LA, LONDON, PARIS and PACFIC RIM BOOK FESTIVAL AWARDS

Robert Uhene Maikai, Editor

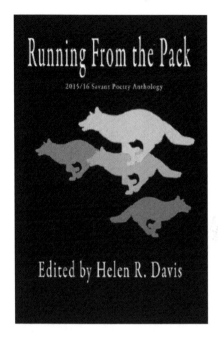

Running from the Pack

2015/16 Savant Poetry Anthology

Helen R. Davis (Editor)

100 pp. 5.25" x 8" Softcover

ISBN 978-0-9963255-5-4

Thirty-five selected poems by fifteen outstanding poets including Dylan DiMarchi, Teuta S. Rizaj, Uhene, Marianne Smith, Danny Smith, Manal Hamad, Thomas Koron, J. Okajima, A. G. Hayes, Kelsea Kennedy, C. P. Little, Helen R. Davis, Doc Krinberg, Kaethe Kauffman and Daniel S. Janik.

PACFIC RIM BOOK FESTIVAL AWARD

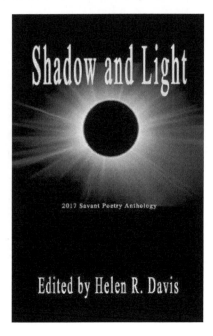

Shadow and Light - 2017 Savant Poetry Anthology
Edited by Helen R. Davis
134 pp. 5.25" x 8" Softcover Pocketbook
ISBN 978-0-9972472-8-2

Sixty-four selected poems by twenty-two outstanding poets including, in order of appearance, Rose Seaquill, Bipul Banerjee, Dr. Mike, Doc Krinberg, Jock Armour, Mr. Ben, Emily Anderson, Marianne Smith, Carolina Casas, Cigeng Zhang, Thomas Koron, Mark Daniel Seiler, Dwight Armbrust Jr, Uhene, Daniel S. Janik, Lonner F. Holden, Sara Hawley, Ihar Kazak, Barbara Bailey, V. Bright Saigal, Ken Rasti and Teuta S. Rizaj.

Robert Uhene Maikai, Editor

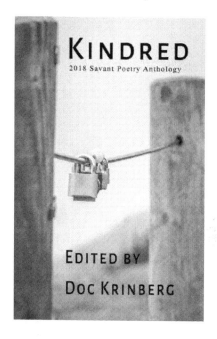

KINDRED - 2018 Savant Poetry Anthology
Edited by Doc Krinberg
110 pp - 5.25" x 8" Softcover
ISBN/EAN 978-0-9994633-0-7

Fifty select poems by nineteen outstanding poets including Dorothy Winslow Wright, Daniel S. Janik, Doc Krinberg, Stacey Lorinn Joy, Bipul Banerjee, Anna Banasiak, Jana Gartung, Hongri Yuan, Cigeng Zhang, Heidi Willson, Kaethe Kauffman, Irtika Kazi, Ihar Kazak, Shikeb Siddiqi, T.W. Behz, Thomas Koron, Uhene, Ken Rasti and Derek Bickerton.

ENTWINED - 2019 Savant Poetry Anthology

Edited by Doc Krinberg

140 pp; 5.25" x 8" Softcover

ISBN/EAN 978-0-9994633-7-6

Sixty-six outstanding poems by twenty-one notable poets including Jean Toyama, Shikeb Siddiqi, Ndaba Sibanda, Thomas Koron, Sahaj Sabharwal, Ulysses Tetu, Bhupesh Chandra Karmakar, Cigeng Zhang, Daniel S. Janik, Karen T. Sisler, Robert Wood, Anna Banasiak, Kierra Donadelle, Ihar Kazak, Stacey Lorinn Joy, V. Bright Saigal, Kaethe Kauffman, Dorothy Winslow Wright, Lonner Holden, Priya Patel and Doc Krinberg.

AN AMAZON GENRE BESTSELLER

Robert Uhene Maikai, Editor

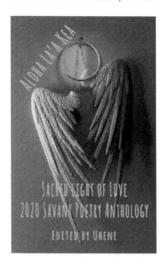

ALOHA LA'A KEA - 2020 Savant Poetry Anthology
Edited by Robert "Uhene" Maikai
225 pp; 5.25" x 8" Softcover
ISBN/EAN 978-0-9996938-6-5

Eighty-six outstanding poems by thirty-five remarkable poets including Greg Dasalla, Garrett Uehara, Moses Pilla, Malia Elliott, Nicole Maika'i-St. Louis, Jay Palompo, Ken Rasti, James Andrade, Dorothy Winslow Wright, Skyla Reyes, Karen Sisler, Hongri Yuan, Daniel S. Janik, Rüdiger Herzing Rückmann, Chuck St. Louis, Michael Lau, Milionea Toluao, Christopher Scott Halicion, Brent Kutara, Uhene, Miranda Zhang, Sidney Esperas, Paul Giovenco, Eddie Aribon, Chino Villa, Cathy A. Schultz, Kimo Dunn, Kaethe Kauffman, Serena Saleh, Cigeng Zhang, Martin Estaban, Mike Patelo, Mark Kempf, Abram Rocky Horner and Conner Maika'i-St. Louis.

*If you enjoyed **Pua La'a Kea**, consider these other fine poetic works from Savant books and Publications:*

Savant Single-Poet Poetry Collections

Footprints, Smiles and Little White Lies by Daniel S. Janik
The Illustrated Middle Earth by Daniel S. Janik
Last and Final Harvest by Daniel S. Janik

Aignos Single-Poet Poetry Collections

Iwana by Alvaro Leiva
Prepositions by Jean Yamaskai Toyama

Robert Uhene Maikai, Editor

As well as these other fine books from
Savant Books and Publications:

Essay, Essay, Essay by Yasuo Kobachi
Aloha from Coffee Island by Walter Miyanari
Footprints, Smiles and Little White Lies by Daniel S. Janik
The Illustrated Middle Earth by Daniel S. Janik
Last and Final Harvest by Daniel S. Janik
A Whale's Tale by Daniel S. Janik
Tropic of California by R. Page Kaufman
Tropic of California (the companion music CD) by R. Page Kaufman
The Village Curtain by Tony Tame
Dare to Love in Oz by William Maltese
The Interzone by Tatsuyuki Kobayashi
Today I Am a Man by Larry Rodness
The Bahrain Conspiracy by Bentley Gates
Called Home by Gloria Schumann
First Breath edited by Z. M. Oliver
The Jumper Chronicles by W. C. Peever
William Maltese's Flicker - #1 Book of Answers by William Maltese
My Unborn Child by Orest Stocco
Last Song of the Whales by Four Arrows
Perilous Panacea by Ronald Klueh
Falling but Fulfilled by Zachary M. Oliver
Mythical Voyage by Robin Ymer
Hello, Norma Jean by Sue Dolleris
Charlie No Face by David B. Seaburn
Number One Bestseller by Brian Morley
My Two Wives and Three Husbands by S. Stanley Gordon
In Dire Straits by Jim Currie
Wretched Land by Mila Komarnisky
Who's Killing All the Lawyers? by A. G. Hayes
Ammon's Horn by G. Amati
Wavelengths edited by Zachary M. Oliver

176

Pua La'a Kea -- Sacred Light of Flower

Communion by Jean Blasiar and Jonathan Marcantoni
The Oil Man by Leon Puissegur
Random Views of Asia from the Mid-Pacific by William E. Sharp
The Isla Vista Crucible by Reilly Ridgell
Blood Money by Scott Mastro
In the Himalayan Nights by Anoop Chandola
On My Behalf by Helen Doan
Chimney Bluffs by David B. Seaburn
The Loons by Sue Dolleris
Light Surfer by David Allan Williams
The Judas List by A. G. Hayes
Path of the Templar—Bk 2 of The Jumper Chronicles by W. C. Peever
The Desperate Cycle by Tony Tame
Shutterbug by Buz Sawyer
Blessed are the Peacekeepers by Tom Donnelly and Mike Munger
Bellwether Messages edited by D. S. Janik
The Turtle Dances by Daniel S. Janik
The Lazarus Conspiracies by Richard Rose
Purple Haze by George B. Hudson
Imminent Danger by A. G. Hayes
Lullaby Moon (CD) by Malia Elliott of Leon & Malia
Volutions edited by Suzanne Langford
In the Eyes of the Son by Hans Brinckmann
The Hanging of Dr. Hanson by Bentley Gates
Flight of Destiny by Francis Powell
Elaine of Corbenic by Tima Z. Newman
Ballerina Birdies by Marina Yamamoto
More More Time by David B. Seabird
Crazy Like Me by Erin Lee
Cleopatra Unconquered by Helen R. Davis
Valedictory by Daniel Scott
The Chemical Factor by A. G. Hayes
Quantum Death by A. G. Hayes and Raymond Gaynor
Big Heaven by Charlotte Hebert
Captain Riddle's Treasure by GV Rama Rao
All Things Await by Seth Clabough
Tsunami Libido by Cate Burns

Robert Uhene Maikai, Editor

Finding Kate by A. G. Hayes
The Adventures of Purple Head, Buddha... by Erik/Forest Bracht
In the Shadows of My Mind by Andrew Massie
The Gumshoe by Richard Rose
In Search of Somatic Therapy by Setsuko Tsuchiya
Cereus by Z. Roux
The Solar Triangle by A. G. Hayes
Shadow and Light edited by Helen R. Davis
A Real Daughter by Lynne McKelvey
StoryTeller by Nicholas Bylotas
Bo Henry at Three Forks by Daniel Bradford
Kindred edited by Gary "Doc" Krinberg
Cleopatra Victorious by Helen R. Davis
Navel of the Sea by Elizabeth McKague
Entwined edited by Gary "Doc" Krinberg
Critical Writing: Stories as Phenomena by Jamie Dela Cruz
Truth and Tell Travel the Solar System by Helen R. Davis
Aloha La'a Kea edited by Robert "Uhene" Maikai
Hawaii Kids Music Vol 1 by Leon and Malia
William Maltese's Flicker - #2 Book of Ascendency by William Maltese

Coming Soon
Hawaii Kids Music Vol 2 by Leon and Malia
The Power of Dance by Setsuko Tsuchiya
I Love Liking You A Lot by Greg Hatala
Retribution by Richard Rose
Shep's Adventures by George Hudson
Lion's Way by Rita Ariyoshi

and from our *avant garde* imprint, **Aignos Publishing:**

The Dark Side of Sunshine by Paul Guzzo
Cazadores de Libros Perdidos by German Barber [Spanish]
The Desert and the City by Derek Bickerton
The Overnight Family Man by Paul Guzzo
There is No Cholera in Zimbabwe by Zachary M. Oliver
John Doe by Buz Sawyers
178

Pua La'a Kea -- Sacred Light of Flower

The Piano Tuner's Wife by Jean Yamasaki Toyama
An Aura of Greatness by Brendan P. Burns
Polonio Pass by Doc Krinberg
Iwana by Alvaro Leiva
University and King by Jeffrey Ryan Long
The Surreal Adventures of Dr. Mingus by Jesus Richard Rodriguez
Letters by Buz Sawyers
In the Heart of the Country by Derek Bickerton
El Camino De Regreso by Maricruz Acuna [Spanish]
Prepositions by Jean Yamasaki Toyama
Deep Slumber of Dogs by Doc Krinberg
Saddam's Parrot by Jim Currie
Beneath Them by Natalie Roers
Chang the Magic Cat by A. G. Hayes
Illegal by E. M. Duesel
Island Wildlife: Exiles, Expats and Exotic Others by Robert Friedman
The Winter Spider by Doc Krinberg
The Princess in My Head by J. G. Matheny
Comic Crusaders by Richard Rose
I'll Remember by Clif McCrady
The City and the Desert by Derek Bickerton
The Edge of Madness by Raymond Gaynor
'Til Then Our Written Love Will Have to Do by Cheri Woods
Honeymoon Forever by R. Page Kaufman